rockschool®

LET'S ROCK

START PLAYING NOW!

GUITAR

www.rslawards.com

rockschool® LET'S ROCK

ACKNOWLEDGEMENTS

Published by Rockschool Ltd. © 2013
Catalogue Number RSK121301
ISBN: 978-1-908920-37-9
Revision 1 | 7 March 2014

AUDIO

Recorded, mixed and mastered at Langlei Studios by Duncan Jordan
Producer: James Uings

MUSICIANS

Stuart Clayton, Neel Dhorajiwala, Noam Lederman, Jon Musgrave, Charlie Griffiths

PUBLISHING

Publishing Manager: James Uings
Editorial Manager: Stephen Lawson
Written by James Uings and Stephen Lawson
Music engraving by Simon Troup and Jennie Troup of Digital Music Art
Logo design by Bryn Reynolds
Proofing: Chris Bird, George Wood and Simon Bradley

SYLLABUS

Syllabus Director: Jeremy Ward
Instrumental specialists: Stuart Clayton, Noam Lederman, James Uings

PRINTING

Printed and bound in the United Kingdom by Caligraving Ltd

PHOTOGRAPHY

Photographer: Adam Gasson
Guitarist: George Wood

DISTRIBUTION

Exclusive Distributors: Music Sales Ltd

CONTACTING ROCKSCHOOL

www.rslawards.com
Telephone: +44 (0)845 460 4747
Email: *info@rslawards.com*

RSL Awarding the Contemporary Arts

CONTENTS

GETTING STARTED

LESSONS

PIECES

EXAMS

WOW!!

WELCOME

Welcome to Let's Rock Guitar!

This book will guide you through the basics of rock and pop guitar playing. It has been designed to build your skills and knowledge as you work through the lessons. The book is split into three main parts: Getting Started, Lessons and Pieces.

GETTING STARTED

The first section of the book contains all the information you will need before you begin your first lesson. This includes a guide to how your instrument works, an introduction to reading music and all the techniques used in the book.

LESSONS

The lessons are split into styles of music with two parts for each style. You will practise musical examples which build up to a final example taken from a piece later in the book. There is also space for teacher feedback at the end of every lesson.

PIECES

Once you have worked your way through the lessons you will be ready to practise and perform your first full pieces of music. You will find these towards the back of the book – one for each style of music that you will learn in the lessons.

There are also three extra pieces which can be played on your own or as part of a band. The other band parts can be found in *Let's Rock Bass* and *Let's Rock Drums* and the full band score is part of your downloadable package.

AUDIO

Every musical example and piece in *Let's Rock Guitar* has two audio tracks that can be downloaded from the Rockschool website. The first is a full track that includes the guitar part along with a full band. The other is a backing track with the guitar taken off so you can play along with the band.

DOWNLOAD

The downloadable content for this book can be downloaded from RSL directly at the following URL:

www.rslawards.com/downloads

When downloading files you will need to input this code when prompted: FC24K4ATD8

The audio files are supplied in MP3 format, the most widely compatible audio format in common usage – MP3s will likely be familiar to anyone with a computer, iPod, smartphone or similar device. Once downloaded you will be able to play them on any compatible device; we hope that you find this extra versatility useful.

GETTING STARTED
INTRODUCTION

This section of *Let's Rock Guitar* contains all the information you will need before you begin your first lesson. Over the next few pages you will find a guide to how your instrument works, all the techniques used throughout the book and an introduction to reading music.

THE GUITAR
A QUICK GUIDE

All you need to know about this amazing instrument

ELECTRIC GUITAR & AMPLIFIER

If you want to play electric guitar you should first plug it into an amplifier (amp). You could play the guitar 'unplugged', but it would be too quiet to hear properly. Here are all the parts of the guitar and amp that you need to know about…

PICKUPS

The pickups have magnets inside that sense the strings' vibrations. These smart devices then turn the vibrations into a signal that can be amplified (made loud) by an amplifier.

FRET BOARD

This is the area on the front of the neck where you place your fingertips.

BRIDGE

The strings are fixed at the body end of the guitar by the bridge. There are two main types: hard-tail and tremolo. A hard-tail bridge keeps the strings fixed against the body, whereas a tremolo bridge lets you raise and lower the pitch of the strings with a tremolo bar.

VOLUME CONTROL

Turn this clockwise (from 0 to 10) to increase the volume of your guitar.

JACK PLUG

Plug a cable in here then plug the other end into your amp.

TONE CONTROLS

Turn these clockwise (from 0 to 10) to increase the brightness of your guitar's sound.

STRINGS

The guitar's sound starts here. When you pluck a string it vibrates, making a note. How high or low the note sounds (its pitch) depends on where you press down on the string.

TUNING PEGS

Turn these to get your strings in tune. The best way to tune your guitar is with an electronic tuner, or if you don't have one of these you could ask your teacher for some help.

FRETS

Frets divide each string into separate notes.

FRET MARKERS

You can use these to quickly work out which fret is which. The following frets are usually marked: 3rd, 5th, 7th, 9th, 12th, 15th, 17th, 19th and 21st.

NECK

The strings are stretched across the length of the neck, which is shaped so you can place your fingers and thumb around it and then play notes.

ACOUSTIC GUITAR

Unlike the electric guitar, the acoustic guitar sounds loud enough on its own, so you shouldn't need an amp. These are the bits you should know about…

1 LARGE BODY

Acoustic guitars have bigger bodies than electric guitars. The body is hollow rather than made of one solid piece of wood. This makes the sound much louder.

2 SOUNDHOLE

This hole on the top of the body works a bit like a loudspeaker. It sends the sound – amplified by the acoustic guitar's large hollow body – out of the body and into the air where it can be heard.

STRAP PINS

Attach a strap to these and you will be able to stand up while playing your guitar.

CABLE Carries a signal from your guitar's pickups to your amp.

VOLUME & GAIN

Use the volume knob (sometimes labelled 'master') to increase the overall volume. Some amps will have a second control marked 'gain'. Turning this up will add a crunchy sound to your guitar's tone.

TONE CONTROLS

These are usually 'bass', 'middle' and 'treble'. Adding more bass makes your guitar sound warmer and fatter. Treble is the opposite: it makes your guitar sound bright and sparkly. Middle is between bass and treble. It's hard to describe tone in words, so make sure you play with all of these controls and hear for yourself once you're plugged into your amp!

PLAYING THE GUITAR

You will need to master these basic techniques to play the songs and examples in this book...

SITTING WITH YOUR GUITAR

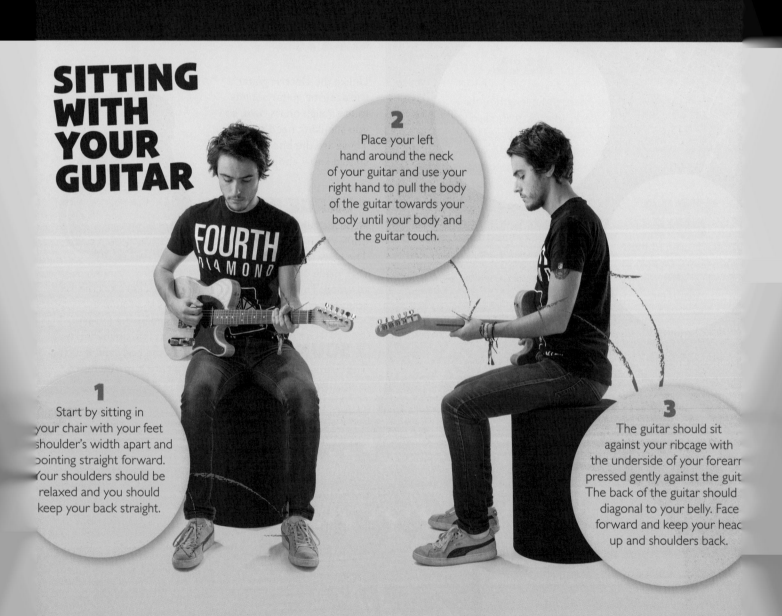

2
Place your left hand around the neck of your guitar and use your right hand to pull the body of the guitar towards your body until your body and the guitar touch.

1
Start by sitting in your chair with your feet shoulder's width apart and pointing straight forward. Your shoulders should be relaxed and you should keep your back straight.

3
The guitar should sit against your ribcage with the underside of your forearm pressed gently against the guitar. The back of the guitar should diagonal to your belly. Face forward and keep your head up and shoulders back.

USING A PICK

1 Take your right hand and turn it so your thumb is pointing upwards – a bit like if you were going to shake someone's hand. Stretch your fingers so they are pointing forward.

2 Curl your fingers back (2a) then place the pick on top of your fingers and put your thumb on top of the pick (2b). Don't squeeze your fingers too much; your hand should stay relaxed.

3 When you pluck a string, only the very end (the tip) should strike the string. To strum more than one string at a time, brush the tip of the pick gently across the surface of the strings.

HOW TO PICK

1 With your right forearm resting lightly on the guitar's body, hold the pick over the bottom (fattest) string. The tip of the pick should be just above the string. Hold the pick firmly between your thumb and index finger but keep your hand relaxed throughout.

2 Move your wrist in a downward motion so that the tip of the pick strikes the string. Try to keep the movement as small as possible so that the pick goes only a few millimetres past the string. This means you won't have to move your pick so far to play the next note.

PLAYING NOTES

1 Place your left hand around the far end of the fretboard and position your thumb in the middle of the back of the neck. Everyone's hands are different, so don't worry if your thumb doesn't line up exactly as shown here. Just make sure you press using the top, not the base, of your thumb.

2 Press your first (pointing) finger on the 1st fret of the B (2nd) string. It should be close to but not on top of the fret.

3 Bring your elbow forward so that your wrist moves closer towards the neck. This will raise your fingers so that they point straight at the fretboard and only the fingertips will come into contact with the strings.

4 Strike the string following the advice in 'How to pick'. Congratulations, you've just played your first note, a C!

HANDY HINT

In this book we will often refer to the left hand as the fretting hand, because it 'frets' the notes of the guitar. The right hand is known as the picking hand. Left-handed players should reverse this.

ONE FINGER PER FRET

As you play through the lessons and pieces in this book you should use what's called the one-finger-per-fret method. This means using your first finger to play the 1st fret, your second to play the 2nd and so on, as shown in the photo above. Notice how each finger is placed close to but not on top of each fret. This method means you can keep your hand more or less in one position and not have to move it around every time you need to play a different note.

HOW TO
READ MUSIC

You'll be reading music in no time with this guide!

TAB

TAB is the most popular type of notation for guitarists because you don't have to learn to read music before you start using it. TAB shows you what notes to play by placing numbers on top of six lines that represent the strings of the guitar. The numbers tell you where to place your fingers on each string. But TAB doesn't show you when to play the notes nor how long each note should last. All of this information can be found on the musical stave…

THE STAVE

The stave appears above the TAB and contains information on what notes to play, when to play them and how long to play them for. The stave consists of five lines. Notes can be placed on any of these lines or any space between the lines.

TEMPO, BARLINES & TIME SIGNATURES

Music is divided into groups of beats called bars. Vertical lines on the stave called barlines show where each bar begins and ends. The symbol with one number on top of another is the time signature. The top number tells you how many beats there are in each bar, while the bottom tells you what kind of beats they are. The time signature below shows there are four quarter notes in each bar, or 4/4 for short. You will learn about quarter notes in your first lesson. The tempo tells you how fast the song is, measured in beats-per-minute.

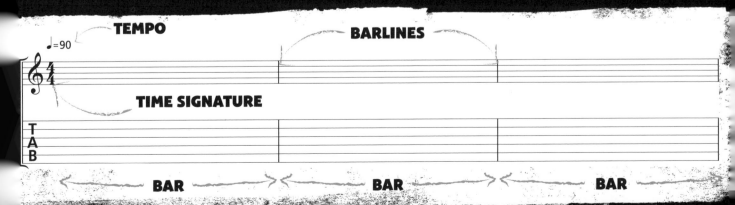

THE CLEF

This is the treble clef. It tells you which note each line and space of the stave represents. There are lots of different kinds of clefs which place the notes on different lines and spaces, but the treble clef is the only one you need to know for guitar.

THE NOTES

The notes that fall on the lines of the stave can be remembered by the phrase 'Every Good Boy Deserves Football' – or you could make up your own. The spaces between the lines can be remembered easily because they spell the word 'FACE'. If you get stuck, try 'Space spells FACE'!

E	G	B	D	F		F	A	C	E
Every	Good	Boy	Deserves	Football			"Face"		

RHYTHM

The rhythms in musical notation are described on the stave by different note heads and stems. These tell you where in the music each note should be played and how long it should be played for. The lessons that follow later in this book will cover different notes and rhythms.

DID YOU KNOW?

Music notation was first used in the Middle East over 3,000 years ago! Instructions for the words and melody of an ancient hymn were discovered in Syria on a clay tablet from around 1400 BC. People in those days used a stylus to carve symbols in wet clay. Once the clay was dry you couldn't make any changes – this was 3,000 years before electronic tablets!

NOTE VALUES

To help you remember the value of each note and rest you will come across in your lessons, we have included the diagrams below. These show the value of each note and rest relative to the others. So, for example, you can see that one whole note is the same length (or value) as four quarter notes...

NOTE VALUES

Whole note			4 beats each
4			
𝅝			

Half-note			2 beats each
2		2	
𝅗𝅥		𝅗𝅥	

Quarter-note			1 beat each
1	1	1	1
𝅘𝅥	𝅘𝅥	𝅘𝅥	𝅘𝅥

Eighth-note							½ beat each
½	½	½	½	½	½	½	½
𝅘𝅥𝅮	𝅘𝅥𝅮	𝅘𝅥𝅮	𝅘𝅥𝅮	𝅘𝅥𝅮	𝅘𝅥𝅮	𝅘𝅥𝅮	𝅘𝅥𝅮

REST VALUES

Whole note rest			4 beats each
4			
𝄻			

Half-note rest			2 beats each
2		2	
𝄼		𝄼	

Quarter-note rest			1 beat each
1	1	1	1
𝄽	𝄽	𝄽	𝄽

Eighth-note rest							½ beat each
½	½	½	½	½	½	½	½
𝄾	𝄾	𝄾	𝄾	𝄾	𝄾	𝄾	𝄾

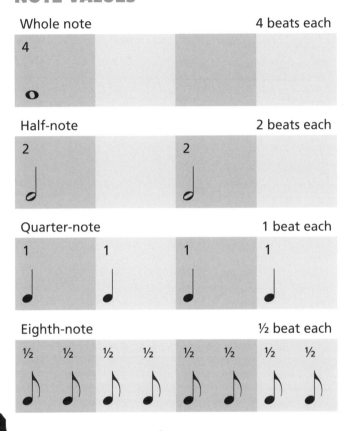

My Notes

LESSONS
INTRODUCTION

Now you understand how your instrument works and know how to read music, it's time for your first music lessons! These are split into different styles of music, with two parts for each style. You will practise short musical examples which build up to a final example at the end of each lesson, which is taken from a piece later in the book.

ROCK PART 1

Your first lesson shows you how to rock out while playing riffs using simple rhythms

DID YOU KNOW?

Jimi Hendrix is considered the greatest guitar player ever. He played his guitar upside down, but reversed the strings so that it played in the same way as your guitar does.

© PETER TARNOFF / RETNA LTD. / CORBIS

WHAT YOU WILL LEARN
☑ Two notes: E & G
☑ What riffs and melodies are
☑ Half & quarter notes

Rock is one of the most popular styles of guitar music. A rock band usually has a singer, one or two guitarists, a bass player and a drummer. The guitarist will often change the sound of their guitar by using the controls on their amp to produce distortion. This helps give the rock band its loud, powerful sound. Led Zeppelin, AC/DC and Foo Fighters are three famous rock groups. Although distorted guitars are a feature of rock music, all the examples found in this lesson can be played on any type of guitar using any sound.

RIFFS & MELODIES

A riff is a short, repeated phrase. Riffs are used in lots of guitar music, especially rock, pop, blues and metal. Songs in these styles are often built on one or two memorable riffs. Melodies are musical phrases that are longer than riffs and are usually sung by a vocalist or played by a lead instrument like the guitar. This lesson introduces riffs.

Don't forget that audio is available for all the musical examples and pieces in this book. Full details on how to access the full band mixes and backing tracks can be found on page 4.

Example 1 — RIFF USING THE E & G NOTES

Example 1 is a riff based on the notes E and G that uses four quarter notes. Place your finger close to but not on top of the fret when you play the G. This will help the note ring clearly without the unwanted noise known as fretbuzz.

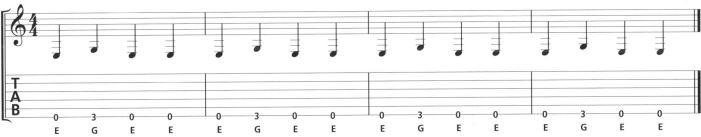

Example 2 — RIFF ACCENTING THE STRONG BEAT OF THE BAR

The first beat of every bar is the strongest, so try to play it slightly harder than the others. Play this example accenting the notes marked 'strong'. You will probably find this happens naturally, but be careful not to play the note too hard.

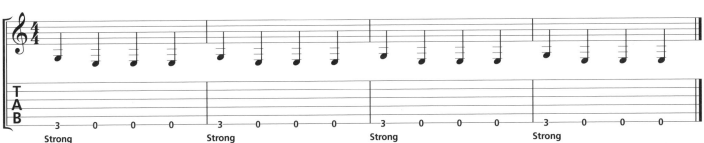

Example 3 — RIFF USING HALF NOTES

Half notes last for two beats each. Two half notes fill one bar. Try counting or tapping your foot to the pulse. This will help you play the notes on the correct beats. The numbers you should count along to the pulse are shown under the music.

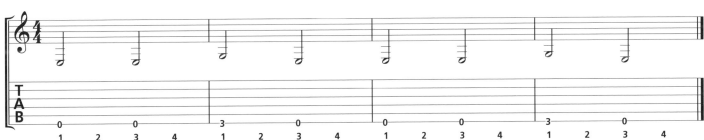

Teacher's Notes

Teacher's Rating

ROCK  PART 2

This lesson introduces two new notes and combines the two note values you learned in part 1

Try tapping your foot on the pulse to help keep your guitar playing in time

You can avoid fretbuzz by making sure you place your fingers close to but not on top of the frets

WHAT YOU WILL LEARN
☑ Two new notes: A & B
☑ How to combine note values
☑ Playing melodies

So far you have played riffs using two notes and two different note values. In Rock Part 2 you will continue to develop your playing and knowledge with three more musical examples (with backing tracks) until you are ready to play two bars of the full piece 'Rock City', which can be found on page 42 of this book.

DID YOU KNOW?

The Gibson Les Paul guitar is played by rock guitarists like Slash, Eric Clapton and Jimmy Page. It is designed to improve sustain, which means that notes last longer than other guitars. This makes it great for guitar solos.

Example 1   RIFF COMBINING HALF NOTES & QUARTER NOTES

Example 1 is a two-bar riff based on the E and G notes you learned in the previous lesson. It combines half notes and quarter notes. This riff is played twice. Tap your foot or count to the pulse to help you play the notes on the correct beat.

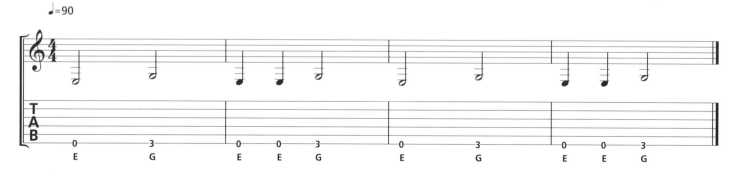

Example 2
MELODY USING FOUR NOTES

Example 2 is a melody that uses a combination of half and quarter notes. It also adds two new notes: A and B. Aim to place your fingers close to but not on top of the frets to help the notes ring clearly without fretbuzz.

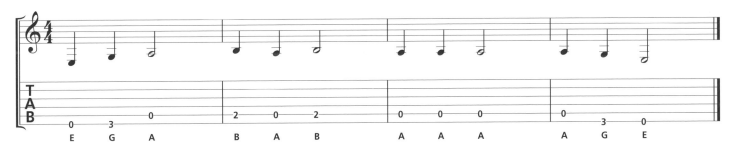

Example 3
MELODY USING FOUR NOTES

This melody uses all the notes and note values you have learned so far. Make sure you play along with the backing track. Once you have played this example, try the extra Do More! examples too.

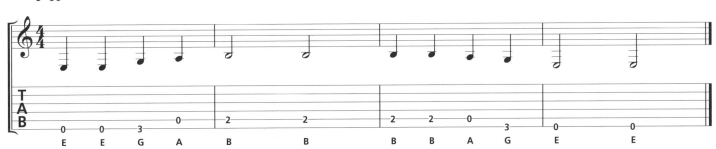

Example 4
'ROCK CITY' BARS 3-4

Example 4 is two bars of the piece 'Rock City', found on page 42. It uses half-note and quarter-note values and four different note names: E, A, G and B. The two bars are played twice to give you more time to practise the example.

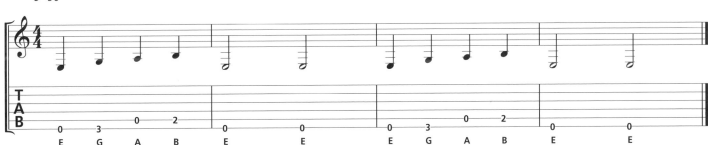

Teacher's Notes

Teacher's Rating

POP PART 1

This introduction to pop guitar covers rests and there are also two new notes for you to learn

DID YOU KNOW?

John Lennon and George Harrison weren't the only guitarists in The Beatles – bassist Paul McCartney could also play guitar. You can hear Paul Mc-Cartney's guitar playing on the popular Beatles song 'Yesterday'.

© RAUCHWETTER / DPA / CORBIS

WHAT YOU WILL LEARN
☑ Quarter-note rests
☑ Two notes: C & F

Pop focuses on the singer and the rest of the instruments support the catchy vocal melodies. Pop bands use keyboards and electronic sounds as well as live instruments like guitar, bass and drums. Guitar isn't usually the main instrument, but plays interesting rhythms and melodies that complement the music. One Direction, Michael Jackson and Katy Perry are three famous pop acts.

RESTS
Silence is a big part of music. What you *don't* play is as important as what you do. However brilliant a musician is, a constant stream of notes can become boring. Breaks in the music allow riffs and melodies to breathe and help create interesting rhythms. In music notation these silences are called rests. All the examples in this lesson use rests that last the same amount of time as a quarter note. These are quarter-note rests.

Don't forget that audio is available for all the musical examples and pieces in this book. Full details on how to access the full band mixes and backing tracks can be found on page 4.

Example 1 — **RIFF WITH RESTS ON BEAT THREE**

There is a rest on beat three of every bar of this riff. Your guitar must be silent for the whole of beat three. Make sure the note played on beat two is silenced (or muted) before beat three starts. Stop the note by releasing pressure on the string.

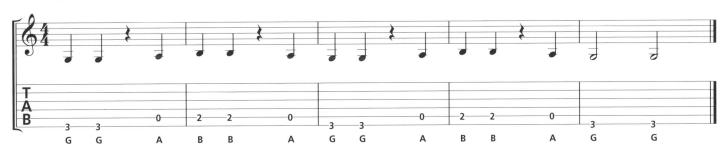

Example 2 — **RIFF USING F NOTE WITH RESTS**

This example introduces the F note and features rests on beats 2 and 4. If you still hear noise after releasing pressure on the strings, place your pick on the string for extra muting.

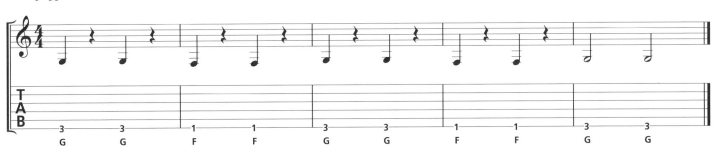

Example 3 — **MELODY USING C NOTE & RESTS**

Example 3 introduces the C note. It also uses rests on beat two of bar 1 and on beat three of bar 3. Remember to use the muting techniques you learned in Examples 1 and 2 to make sure all the notes last for the correct amount of time.

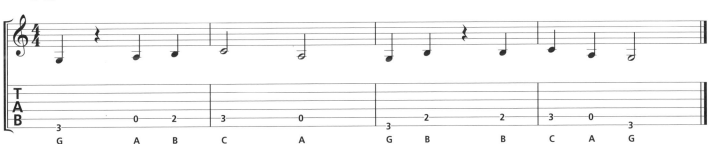

Teacher's Notes

Teacher's Rating

POP  PART 2

Pop Part 2 builds on what you learned in Part 1 and introduces a new note name and a new note value

You can mute the open D string by gently resting your fretting hand on the string

Make sure you download the backing tracks so you can practise playing along with a band!

WHAT YOU WILL LEARN
- ☑ The D note
- ☑ Whole notes
- ☑ A section of a full piece

DID YOU KNOW?

The last lesson showed you how to play riffs and melodies that included four different notes and quarter-note rests. In Pop Part 2 you will learn a new note and a new note value. When you have played through the first three examples in this lesson you'll be ready to try four bars of the full piece 'Party People' on page 43.

The Fender Stratocaster is used in both rock and pop music because it offers a wide range of tones in one guitar. It has three pickups, each with its own unique sound. A switch lets you select either of these as well as two other sounds. Five in one!

Example 1   MELODY WITH a D NOTE

This melody uses the rests you learned in Part 1 and includes the new note D. Remember to play to the backing track as this will help keep you in time with the pulse and get you ready to play in a band.

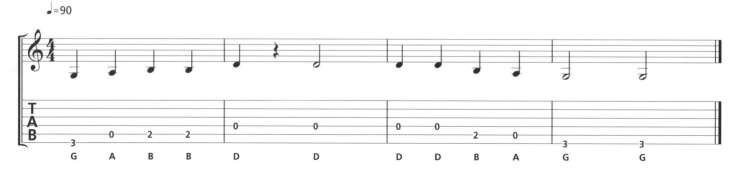

Example 2 — MELODY USING WHOLE NOTES

Whole notes last for four beats and fill up a *whole* bar. This melody uses whole notes. Make sure you count or tap your foot to the pulse. This will make sure that the notes last for the correct amount of time and stop you playing the next note too soon.

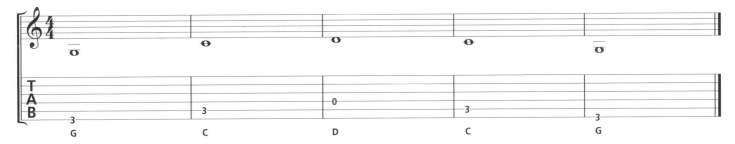

Example 3 — RIFF COMBINING NOTE VALUES

Example 3 is a pop riff that combines all of the note values you have learned so far in this book. Look closely at the value of each note and rest and make sure they last (or that your guitar is silent) for the correct amount of time.

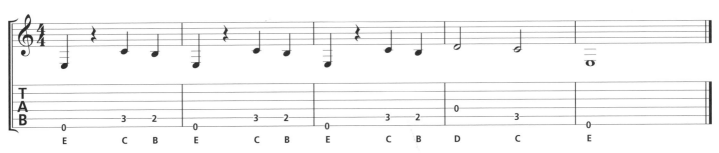

Example 4 — 'PARTY PEOPLE' BARS 13–16

Now it's time to combine all that you've learned in these pop lessons by playing four bars of the piece 'Party People'. It uses quarter notes, half notes and whole notes. It also uses five of the notes you have learned so far.

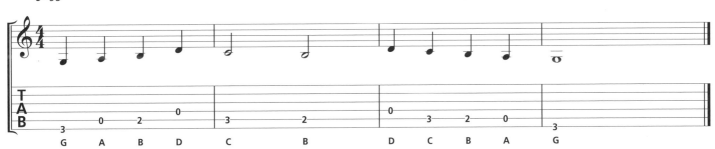

Teacher's Notes

Teacher's Rating

COUNTRY

PART 1

This country lesson shows you how to play melodies that use higher pitched notes and two-beat rests

DID YOU KNOW?

Brad Paisley is a huge country music star and an excellent guitar player. He plays a Fender Telecaster guitar with a paisley pattern on its body. *Paisley,* **get it?!**

WHAT YOU WILL LEARN
☑ Two notes: new E & F
☑ Half-note rests
☑ Octaves

Country began in America but is now popular all over the world. A country band is usually made up of a singer, bass player, drummer, keyboardist and one or two guitarists. Country guitarists play either electric or acoustic guitar. They often play simple chords (a chord is two or more notes played at the same time) and melodies that complement the vocals. However, country guitarists are skilful musicians and are capable of playing fast and impressive lead guitar too. Johnny Cash, Taylor Swift and Dolly Parton are three of the most famous country stars.

OCTAVES

So far you have learned seven notes: E, F, G, A, B, C and D. The next note you will learn is another E note. This has the same sound as the E note you learned in the first rock lesson, but this E sounds higher. The second E is said to be an octave (Latin for eighth) higher than the first because they are separated by eight notes of a scale.

Don't forget that audio is available for all the musical examples and pieces in this book. Full details on how to access the full band mixes and backing tracks can be found on page 4.

Example 1 — MELODY USING E NOTE

This melody adds an E note that's an octave (eight notes of a scale) higher than the one you have already learned. Remember to place your fingers close to but not on top of the fret to avoid fretbuzz.

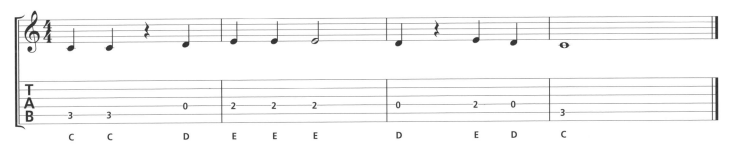

Example 2 — MELODY USING HALF-NOTE RESTS

This melody introduces the half-note rest, which lasts for two beats. Make sure you count the pulse ("1 2 3 4") along with the music to make sure you play the notes on the correct beats.

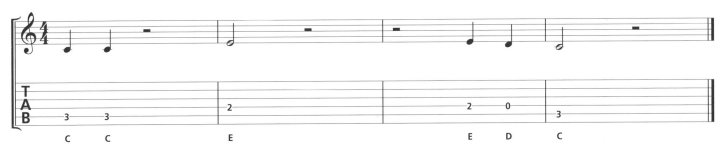

Example 3 — MELODY WITH F NOTE & TWO-BEAT REST

This example introduces the F note. It also uses half-note rests. Note that the two-beat rest in bar 2 is written as two quarter-note rests. This makes it easier to see where the middle of the bar is.

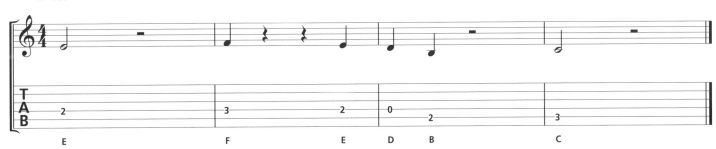

Teacher's Notes

Teacher's Rating

COUNTRY
PART 2

Your second country lesson introduces dotted notes, three-beat rests, and two new notes

You can mute the open G string either by gently resting your fretting hand on the string or...

...by bringing your pick (plectrum) to rest on the string. You can combine both methods

WHAT YOU WILL LEARN
☑ Two new notes: G & A
☑ Dotted notes
☑ Three-beat rests

When a dot is placed after a note the length of the note is changed so that it lasts for its original length plus half of this value again. A dotted half note would last for three beats (two beats + one beat). This lesson features the dotted half note and the three-beat rest as well as two new notes.

DID YOU KNOW?

The Fender Telecaster was the first electric guitar with a solid body that sold in large numbers. It was invented by a man called Leo Fender and went on sale in 1950, known then as the Broadcaster. Its name was changed to Telecaster in 1952.

Example 1   MELODY USING G NOTE

This example uses the half-note rests you learned in Part 1 and adds the G note. It's a good opportunity to practise everything you learned in the first country lesson while learning a new note.

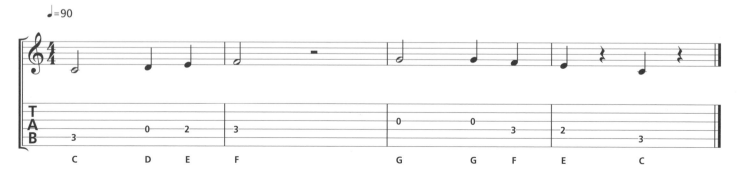

Example 2 — MELODY USING DOTTED HALF NOTE

The dotted half note lasts for three beats ("1 2 3"). Count or tap your foot to the pulse so that you play the quarter note on beat four at the correct time.

♩=95

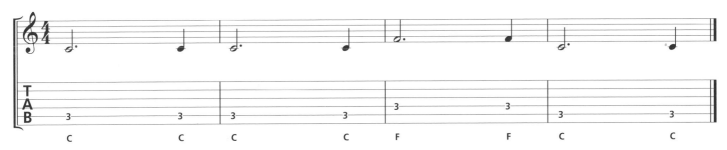

Example 3 — MELODY USING THE A NOTE

This melody introduces the A note and has rests that last for three beats. These are written using half-note and quarter-note rests so you can see where the middle of the bar is.

♩=95

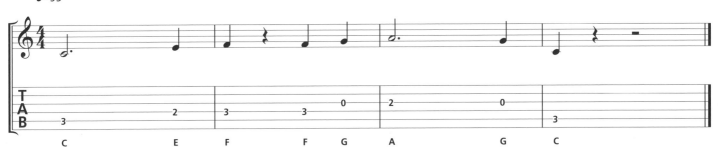

Example 4 — 'ROAD TO NASHVILLE' BARS 5-8

This is four bars of the piece 'Road To Nashville' on page 44. There are lots of different rhythms and rests in these bars, so work through the example slowly and make sure all the notes last for the correct amount of time.

♩=90

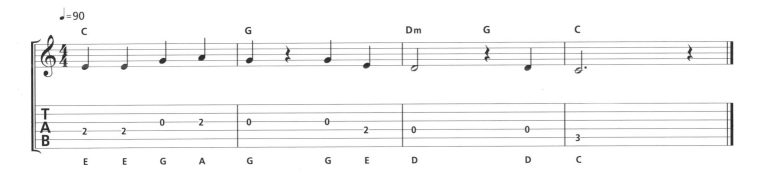

Teacher's Notes

Teacher's Rating

METAL PART 1

This metal lesson will teach you how to make heavy sounds using powerchords

DID YOU KNOW?

Dimebag Darrell was the guitarist for the metal band Pantera. By the time he was 18 he had won all the guitar competitions in Texas and was banned from entering again!

WHAT YOU WILL LEARN
☑ What powerchords are
☑ Two powerchords: E5 & A5

Metal is a dark and intense style of music that usually features two guitarists, a singer, a drummer and a lesss player. The guitarists use lots of distortion for a heavy sound and play riffs that can be slow and powerful or fast and complex. Metal lead guitar is skilful with lots of flashy techniques. Black Sabbath, Metallica and Iron Maiden are three famous metal bands.

POWERCHORDS

A chord is two or more notes played at the same time. Some chords will have six notes and use every string on the guitar. A powerchord is a two- or three-note chord (in this book they are two-note chords). Powerchords get their name because they have a big, powerful sound. When the guitar has a distorted tone a six-note chord can sound messy, which is good for some styles but not for others. Powerchords work well because they provide a powerful yet clear sound that's perfect for rock, metal and punk.

Don't forget that audio is available for all the musical examples and pieces in this book. Full details on how to access the full band mixes and backing tracks can be found on page 4.

Example 1 — HOW TO MAKE A POWERCHORD

A powerchord is written as a chord name (e.g. A or E) followed by the number 5. The note that the chord gets its name from is known as the root note. The '5' is five notes above the root note, so you get 'A5', 'E5' etc.

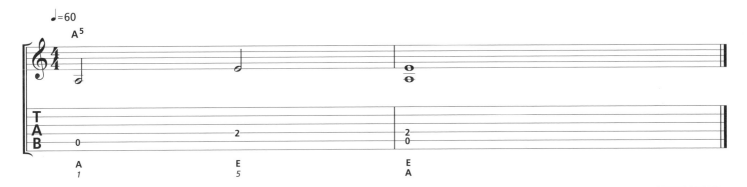

Example 2 — RIFF USING A5 POWERCHORD

Use your first finger to hold down the E note then strike the A and D strings with a single downstroke. Make sure you play only the strings that are notated.

Example 3 — RIFF USING E5 & A5 POWERCHORDS

The E5 chord features the E and B notes. Although the rhythms are half notes, you will have to take your fingers off the chord slightly earlier than shown in the music to change the chord.

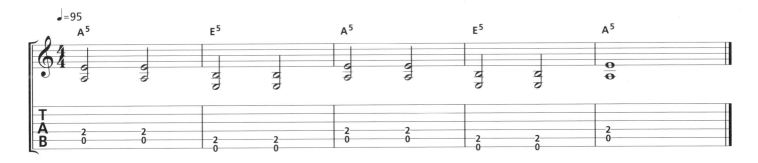

Teacher's Notes

Teacher's Rating

METAL

PART 2

In your second metal lesson you will learn a new note which uses an important musical symbol

You should play the F note on the E string with your first finger...

...and the F# is the next note on the string, so it should be played with your second finger

WHAT YOU WILL LEARN

☑ Sharps

☑ The F# note

☑ What key signatures are

W hen a sharp sign (#) is placed in front of a note, the note is played one fret higher than usual (and sounds higher in pitch). An F note is played on the 1st fret of the E string and an F# is played on the 2nd fret of the same string. This sharp sign is one of a group of musical signs known as accidentals.

DID YOU KNOW?

The 'superstrat' was the first guitar designed specially for the demands of metal players. Jackson's Soloist went on sale in 1981 and offered some of the features of Fender and Gibson guitars in one instrument.

Example 1	RIFF USING F# NOTE

This example introduces the F# note. Notice how the sharp sign is placed before the note on the stave. There are three F# notes in bar 3 of this example. The sharp sign is written only before the first sharp note in each bar.

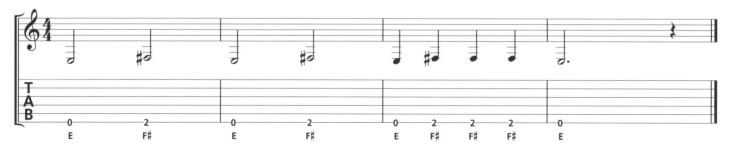

♩=105

Example 2 — RIFF USING A KEY SIGNATURE

If a piece uses F♯ notes all the way through without any F notes (like here), the composer will save writing lots of F♯ notes in the music by writing an F♯ on the top line of the stave at the start of every line of music. This is an example of a key signature.

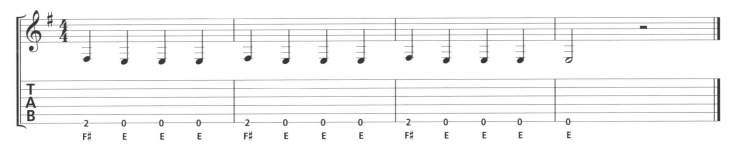

Example 3 — RIFF COMBINING POWERCHORDS & SINGLE NOTES

Metal songs often combine powerchords and single notes. This example gives you a chance to practise switching between the two. The **N.C.** symbol lets you know that **no chord** is being played.

Example 4 — 'LEAD BOOTS' BARS 13-16

These four bars are taken from the piece on page 45. The example combines powerchords and single notes. Once you have played it several times try hitting the strings harder. This will help you get the heavy sound that metal is famous for.

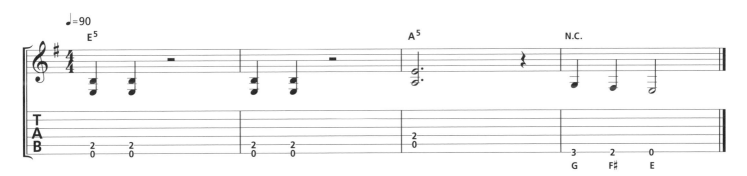

Teacher's Notes

Teacher's Rating

INDIE PART 1

In this introduction to indie you will learn three new notes and play them with a new picking technique

DID YOU KNOW?

Oasis's guitar player Noel Gallagher was a guitar hero in the 1990s. Epiphone named a guitar after one of his songs. But Noel describes his playing as "average at best". Really?!

WHAT YOU WILL LEARN
☑ Three new notes: B, C & D
☑ Alternate picking

The name 'indie' is short for independent because indie records were originally released on small, *independent* record labels rather than bigger major labels. An indie band usually has a singer, one or two guitarists, a drummer and a bass player. The guitarists play clever guitar parts based on chords. They sometimes play solos, but usually play parts that fit the song. The Smiths, Oasis and Arctic Monkeys are all famous indie bands.

PICKING DIRECTIONS
Until now you have probably played every note and chord using only downstrokes. These have a strong sound and the notes in a phrase will sound at a similar volume because you are using the same technique to play them. The problem is that you have to bring the pick back past the string to re-pick it. This wastes time and can make it hard to play lots of notes one after the other. Alternating between downstrokes and upstrokes will help you to play more quickly and fluently.

Don't forget that audio is available for all the musical examples and pieces in this book. Full details on how to access the full band mixes and backing tracks can be found on page 4.

Example 1 — MELODY USING B & C NOTES

This example introduces two new notes: B and C. As well as the location of the new notes, pay attention to the rests in bars 3 and 4 and make sure the notes and rests last the correct amount of time.

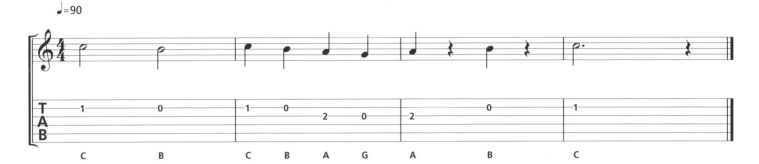

Example 2 — MELODY USING ALTERNATE PICKING

You should play this melody using alternate picking. Play the first note with a downstroke then alternate between downstrokes (⊓) and upstrokes (V). The musical symbols for these pick directions are above the notation to help you.

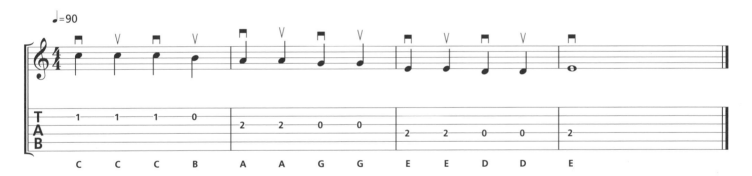

Example 3 — MELODY USING ALTERNATE PICKING & D NOTE

The first note of each new bar should be played with a downstroke even if the note before it was also a downstroke (this will happen if there is an odd number of notes in a bar). This will make the first beat of the bar sound stronger.

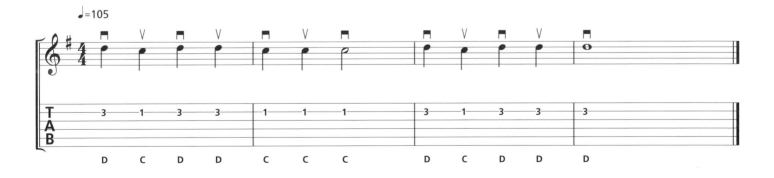

Teacher's Notes

Teacher's Rating

INDIE PART 2

In your second indie lesson you will learn your first three-note chord and play a rhythm guitar part

When this D note is followed by the open E string, stop playing it by releasing pressure on it

Your first three-note chord is played by pressing down only on the B string

WHAT YOU WILL LEARN
☑ A new note: E on the high E string
☑ A new chord: C

You already know two-note powerchords. In this lesson you will play your first three-note chord: C major. Major chords have a bright, happy sound and are usually shortened to letter names, so instead of C major you will see only the letter C above the music. So far you have played melodies and riffs. A part that uses mostly chords is a rhythm guitar part.

DID YOU KNOW?

Effects pedals are used by guitarists to change the sound of their guitars. Distortion is one of the most popular effects. Blur guitarist Graham Coxon used a ProCo Rat distortion on Blur's 'Song 2'. You can hear the effect in the song's chorus.

Example 1   MELODY USING B, C & D NOTES

This melody is a good chance to go back over everything you learned in the last lesson. Remember to tap your foot or count to the pulse to help play the notes in the right place in the bar. Mute the strings in the rests using both your hands.

♩=85

```
B   C     D D C B   A     B A G
```
TAB:
```
0   1   3 3 1 0       0     2   0
          2               2
```

Example 2 — MELODY USING E NOTE

You could leave your finger on the D note in bar 2 to make the part easier to play, but this would mean the D and E notes sounding together instead of one at a time. To avoid this, make sure you stop pressing on the D note as you play the E.

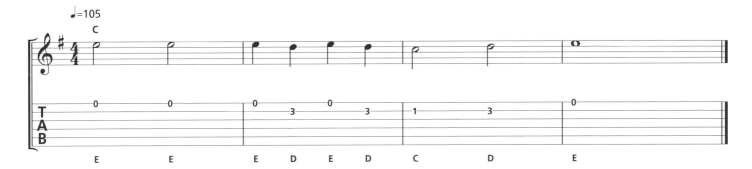

Example 3 — RHYTHM PART USING C CHORD

To play this chord you need only your first finger to fret the C because the other notes are open strings. Arch your finger to avoid touching the E string and stopping it ringing. Brush your pick lightly across the strings so all three notes sound at once.

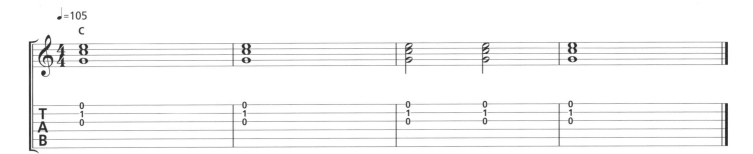

Example 4 — 'PARKA LIFE' BARS 5-8

These fours bars are from the piece 'Parka Life' on page 46. After playing the C note at the start of bar 4 keep your finger pressed down and strum the two extra open strings to make the C chord.

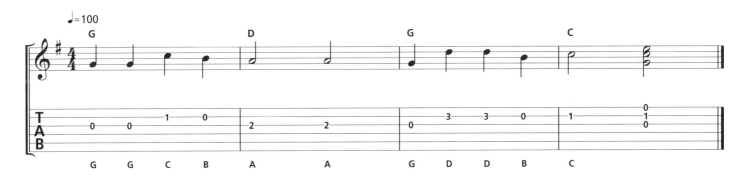

Teacher's Notes

Teacher's Rating

HIP HOP PART 1

In your first hip hop lesson you will learn how to change chords quickly and smoothly

DID YOU KNOW?

Rage Against The Machine's guitarist Tom Morello used his guitar to copy the sounds of a hip hop DJ. One of the best places to hear these effects is the song 'Bulls On Parade'.

WHAT YOU WILL LEARN
☑ Two new notes: G & F#
☑ A new chord: G
☑ How to change chords

Most hip hop music is based on sampling. Sampling is taking a part of a recording and making a new piece of music with it. This was first done in the 1970s by DJs in New York who wanted to extend certain parts of the records they played which were popular with dancers. Since then hip hop musicians have used a mixture of live instruments and machines called samplers to produce songs that use short, catchy ideas that are repeated, usually throughout the whole of a song. Eminem, Will Smith and Jay Z are some famous hip hop artists.

CHANGING CHORDS
So far you have played only one three-note chord, C. In this lesson you will learn a new one, G. The secret to changing smoothly from one chord to another is to think about changing chord a beat or two before the actual change. Picture the shape of the next chord and where on the fretboard your finger must go to play the chord.

Don't forget that audio is available for all the musical examples and pieces in this book. Full details on how to access the full band mixes and backing tracks can be found on page 4.

Example 1 — RIFF USING G & F# NOTES

Play the F# with your second finger and the G with your third finger. This puts your fingers in the correct position if you have to play the 1st fret (using your first finger) or the 4th fret (using your fourth). This is called one-finger-per-fret.

Example 2 — RHYTHM PART WITH G CHORD

Make sure you are holding the pick so only the tip is showing. When strumming, move your wrist smoothly across the strings so the tip brushes the strings without digging in between them. The three notes should sound together, not one at a time.

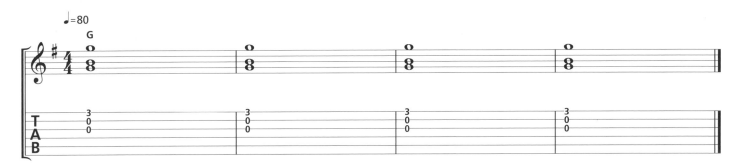

Example 3 — RHYTHM PART WITH TWO CHORDS

This example is an opportunity to practise changing chords, which can be tricky at first. Try practising without the backing track until your chord changes are smooth, then try again with the backing track.

Teacher's Notes

Teacher's Rating

HIP HOP PART 2

In your final lesson you will learn about a new type of chord and change between three chords

This easy version of the E minor chord is played with only one finger pressing on a string

This G chord is also a simplified version which you shouldn't find too difficult to play

WHAT YOU WILL LEARN
- ☑ Your first minor chord
- ☑ Four-note chords
- ☑ A three-chord progression

Your final lesson introduces your first minor chord: E minor, marked 'Em' in the notation ('m' stands for minor). Minor chords have very different qualities from major chords because unlike major chords, which are bright and happy sounding, minor chords have a sad sound. Example 2 demonstrates this.

DID YOU KNOW?

Many hip hop songs sample funk music. This is a dancey style of music that was popular in the 1970s. Lots of funk songs use an effect called wah wah, which copies the effect of opening and closing your mouth to talk.

Example 1   RHYTHM PART WITH E MINOR CHORD

This E minor chord has four notes instead of three. The chord is still made up of only three notes (E, G and B); however, the E note is repeated. It is an octave higher than the root note (i.e. the note that gives the chord its name).

♩=100

Em

(music notation and TAB)

Example 2 — RHYTHM PART WITH E MINOR & G MAJOR

In this example you will practise changing between E minor and G. The E note in the E minor chord should be played with your second finger. Use your third finger to play the G note of the G chord.

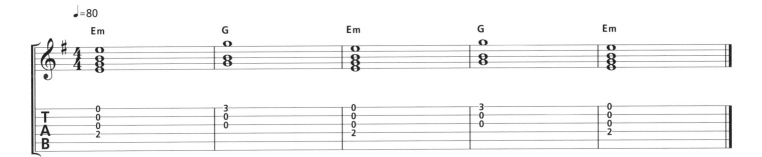

Example 3 — 'REPRESENT' BARS 9-16

This example is taken from the piece 'Represent', which you will find on page 47. It features three chords. Remember to play the top four strings of your guitar for the E minor but only the highest sounding three strings for the C and G.

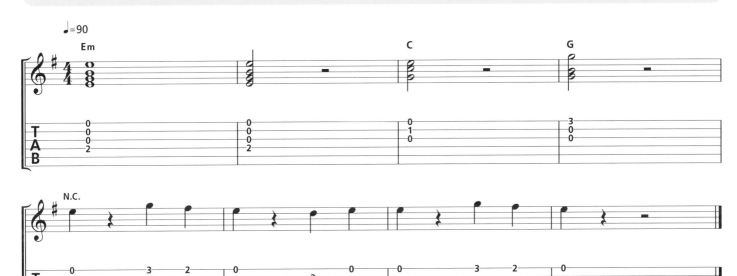

Teacher's Notes

Teacher's Rating

My Notes

PIECES
INTRODUCTION

Now that you have worked your way through the lessons and learned how to play your instrument, you are ready to perform your first full pieces of music. You will find them all in this section – one for each style of music you learned in your lessons.

There are also three extra pieces which can be played on your own or as part of a band. The other band parts can be found in *Let's Rock Bass* and *Let's Rock Drums* and the full band score is part of your downloadable package.

ROCK
'ROCK CITY'

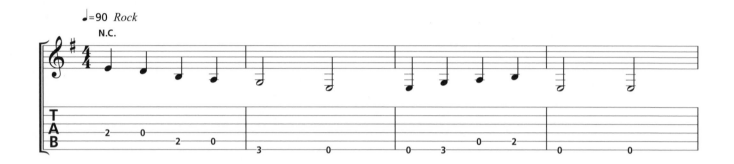

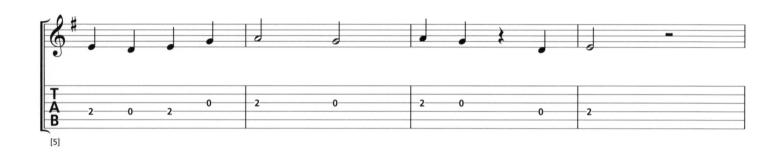

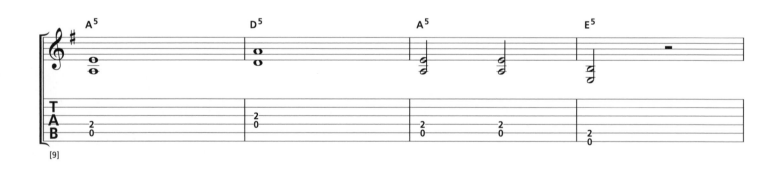

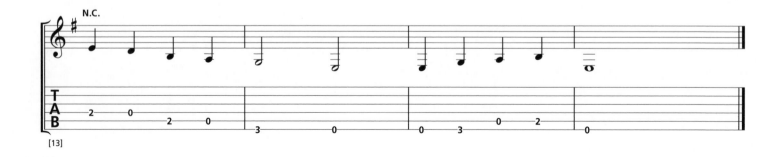

POP
'PARTY PEOPLE'

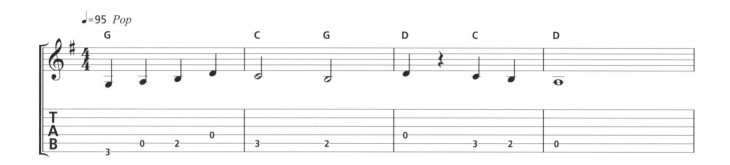

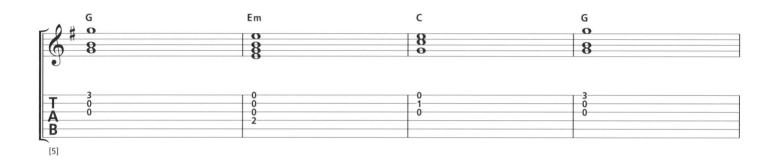

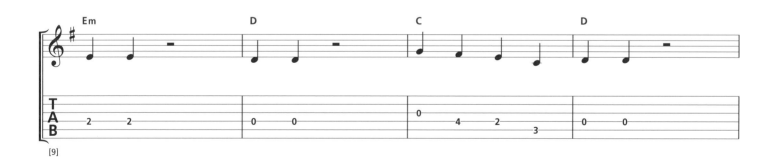

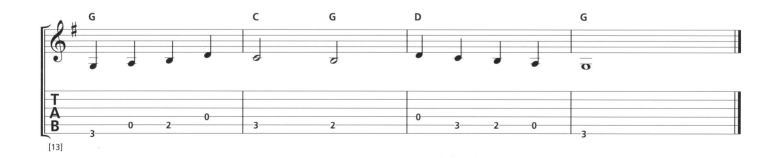

COUNTRY
'ROAD TO NASHVILLE'

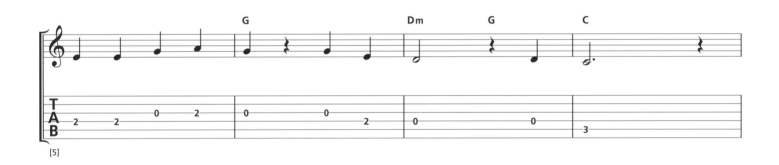

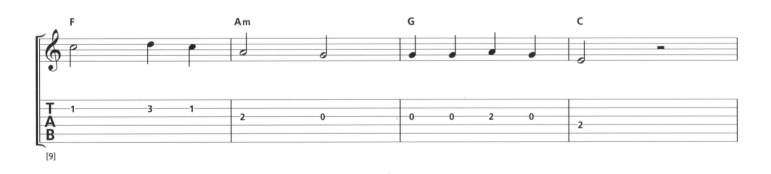

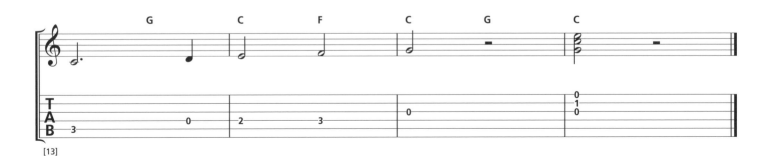

METAL
'LEAD BOOTS'

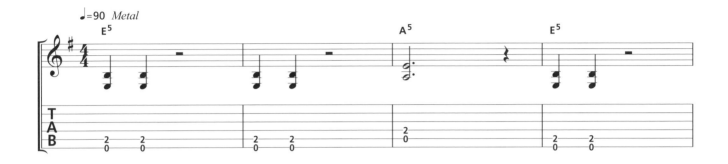

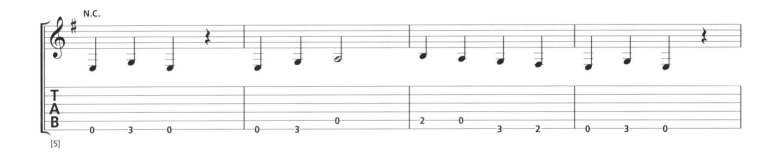

[5]

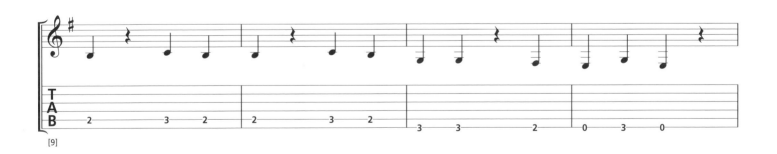

[9]

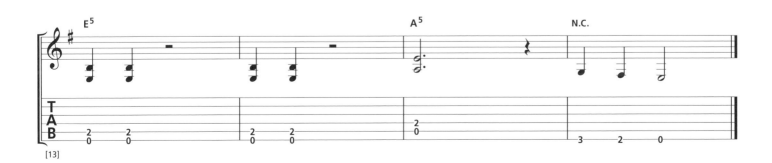

[13]

INDIE
'PARKA LIFE'

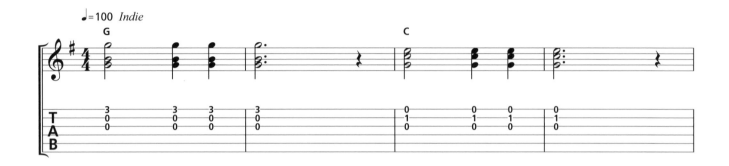

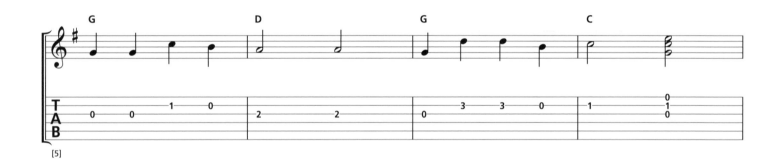

[5]

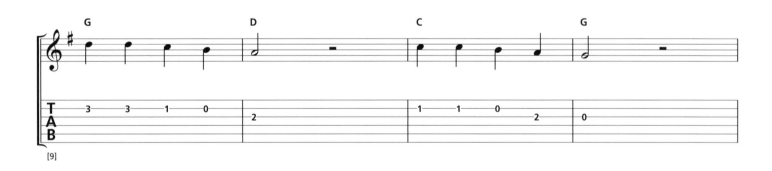

[9]

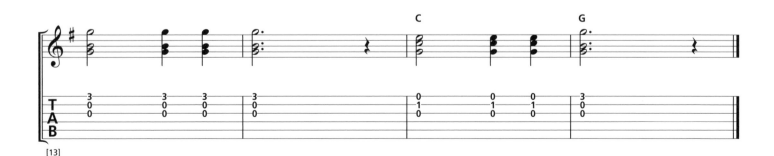

[13]

HIP HOP
'REPRESENT'

[5]

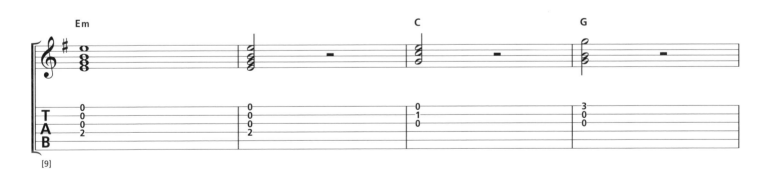

[9]

[13]

ROCK
'OVERLOAD'

♩=90 *Rock*

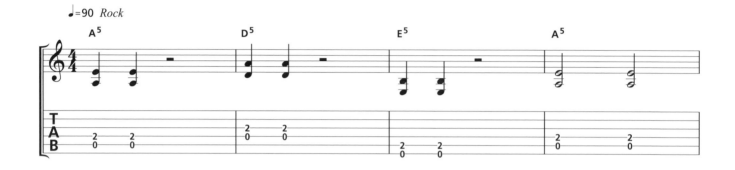

[5]

[9]

[13]

METAL
'SLAM'

♩=90 *Metal*

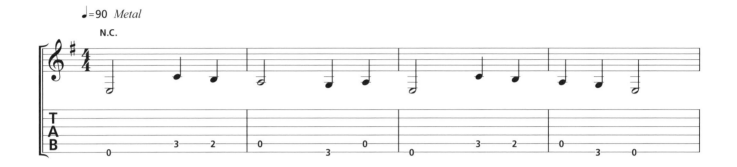

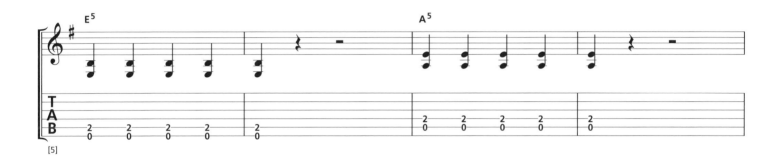

[5]

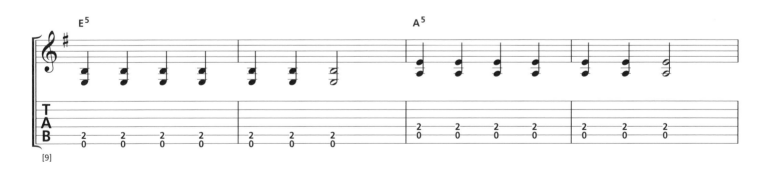

[9]

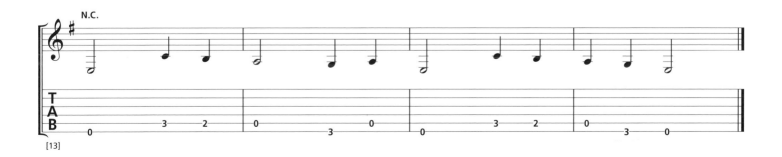

[13]

INDIE
'UNDER THE RADAR'

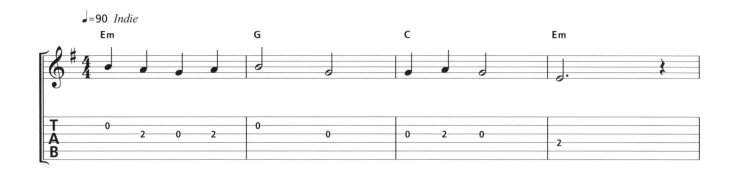

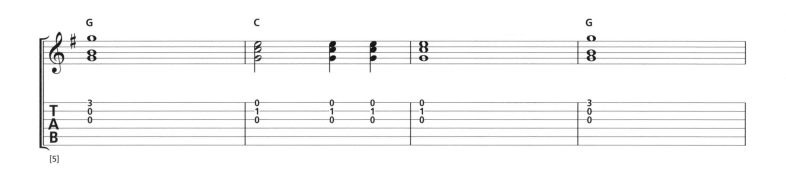

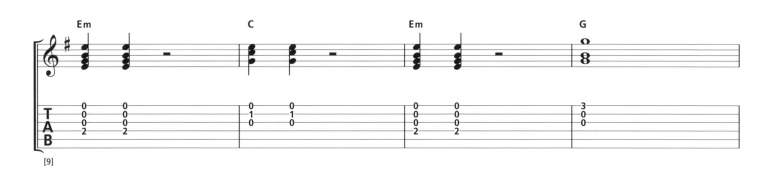

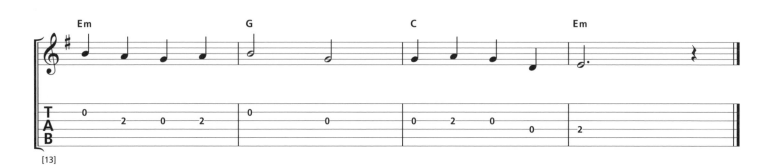

Exam Time!

THE ROCKSCHOOL PREMIERE EXAM

The pieces in this book can now be performed in an examination which is fully accredited just like every other Rockschool grade exam. There are no tests or technicals, just five performance pieces, making it the ideal introduction to Rockschool examinations. Entering a Rockschool exam is easy. You can enter online at *www.rslawards.com* or by downloading and filling in an exam entry form. The full Rockschool examination terms and conditions as well as exam periods and current fees are available from our website or by calling +44 (0)845 460 4747.

THE ROCKSCHOOL PREMIERE EXAM	
ELEMENT	PASS
Performance Piece 1	12+ out of 20
Performance Piece 2	12+ out of 20
Performance Piece 3	12+ out of 20
Performance Piece 4	12+ out of 20
Performance Piece 5	12+ out of 20
TOTAL MARKS	60%+